The Rhythm of It
Poetry's Hidden Dance

The Rhythm of It
Poetry's Hidden Dance

by Anita Sullivan

Shanti Arts Publishing
Brunswick, Maine

The Rhythm of It — Poetry's Hidden Dance

Copyright © 2019 Anita Sullivan

All rights reserved. No part of this book may be used or reproduced in any manner whatsoever without the written permission of the publisher.

Published by Shanti Arts Publishing
Cover and interior design by Shanti Arts Designs

Shanti Arts LLC
Brunswick, Maine
www.shantiarts.com

Printed in the United States of America

All images, including cover, by Imelda Almqvist
www.shaman-healer-painter.co.uk

Brigit Pegeen Kelly, "Of Ancient Origins and War" from *Song*. Copyright © 1995 by Brigit Pegeen Kelly. Reprinted with the permission of The Permissions Company, LLC on behalf of BOA Editions Ltd., boaeditions.org.

"Elegy with a Bridle in Its Hand" from *Elegy* by Larry Levis. © 1997. Reprinted by permission of the University of Pittsburgh Press.

"Micro-minutes on Your Way to Work" by Brenda Hillman. Originally published in Poem-a-Day on May 2, 2018. Copyright © 2018 by Brenda Hillman. Reprinted by permission of Brenda Hillman and the Academy of American Poets, www.poets.org.

ISBN: 978-1-951651-03-9 (softcover)
ISBN: 978-1-951651-04-6 (digital)

Library of Congress Control Number: 2019953829

*for my sons,
Patrick and Timothy*

Contents

Images	9
Preface	11
Tai Chi Time	15
The Pulse	19
Why Rhythm and Not Something Else Instead or Also	23
About Proportional Symmetry	29
Discovering a Proportional Rhythm in an Actual Poem	33
The Walking of It	37
More Deeply into Proportional Rhythm	43
A Nod to Whim	49
Rhythm Revisited	57
The Silence of It	65
We Spin	71
Smuggling the Poem Across	77
Poetic Logic	81
Speech Rhythm as Perpetual Mystery — I	85
Speech Rhythm as Perpetual Mystery — II	89
Poetry and Ritual	95
Plain Speech	99
Conclusion	107
Notes	
Endnotes	111
Poetry References	112
Bibliography	114
About the Author	117

Images

The author extends her heartfelt gratitude to Imelda Almqvist for the use of her extraordinary images in this book. The titles of these images are:

Dancers Surrounded by Batak Script	14
Hand in Hand	18
Conductor Petroglyph Inspired	22
Bird Dancer #2	28
Ice Stunning, Creek, 22 February	32
Wave Dancer #3	36
Making Sounds #2	42
Ice Winner When Ice Smiles!	48
Antlered Woman on Barn	56
Moon's Watery Nature	64
Serpent's Egg (also on cover)	70
Film 2016 Rock Art 2	76
Two Moons, 20 February 2019	80
Ice Council of Creatures	84
Making Sounds #2	88
Human Lyre Petroglyph Inspired #2	94
Fishes Singing #2	98
Serpent's Egg	106

Preface

> The Sanskrit **aksara**[1] belongs to that narrow circle of words like **brahman**, where an ungovernable drift of meanings overwhelms a hypothetical first meaning — hypothetical because eventually we begin to wonder if there is such a meaning. . . .
>
> — Roberto Calasso

I'D LIKE TO PRESENT A SERIES OF SHORT OBSERVATIONS on rhythm in poetry. Each essay carries some aspect of that subject, which of course has had centuries to lose itself in an "ungovernable drift of meanings," so that even trying to decide what should be included in a decent summary narrative, seems impossible. Rather than ponderous discourse or flimsy sketch, I'd like this collection to be perceived as a crystal with many facets: you step up and gaze deeply into each one as if it were complete in itself, each time stepping back to look again upon the gem in its entirety before placing yourself before the next facet. The process is cumulative: as your perceptions shift back and forth between the parts and the whole, understanding builds slowly inside you in at least three dimensions simultaneously.

This is the way many ancient religions dispersed

their teachings into the souls of their acolytes. By going round and round a circle of ideas, each of which overlapped the two on either side, the acolyte gradually built up a new breadth and depth of understanding, achieved by swinging between facet and stone. This is the method still used by gnostics and mystics to offer a way to enlightenment; it is a procedure that allows an actual transfer of knowledge, not simply a piling up of raw information.

Anita Sullivan

Tai Chi Time

TODAY IN TAI CHI CLASS, WHILE WE STAND QUIETLY waiting to begin, I find myself noticing the soft digital ticking of the wall clock. It's a good clock, barely audible most days because its small functional intrusions are readily absorbed into the larger background soundscape that includes the furnace fan, doors opening and closing, voices in the hallway, our collective breathing. But now — did something change? — it sounds exactly like stealthy footsteps on leaves: "pad-pad" instead of "tick-tick," as if, like Pinocchio, our little mechanical device has turned into something real, at last. I smile and relax, feeling immersed in a soft cushioning of natural elements – my classmates, our teacher, the enormous clerestory windows high above us, the hidden blue of the April morning light, and someone out there tiptoeing through a forest.

But as the dozen of us begin to move together into the first part of the form, the clock seems to grow louder, like a single shoe going round and round in a distant clothes drier, drawing attention to itself for no useful reason.

I squint. *The clock has no rhythm!* I realize suddenly. This almost causes me to forget the sharp turn for "white crane spreads its wings." I narrow my concentration back to my body and to the directives that are pulling it forward, urging it to flow through an austere pattern of gestures that over the past four years have become a basic set of motion tendencies within my muscles, nerves, and bones. I feel as if I have been slowly extending my awareness through a deeply complex root system that grows more slender and fine and numerous at its very tips, until it merges with the soil itself. Its thread-like tendrils in the front lines are the ones that daily make the thousands of choices that determine the nature of my future self.

The clock's metric voice, by contrast, is quite predictable, and therefore useless here. Relentlessly, it interrupts the air, the silence, sketching out a two-dimensional symmetry that the vast world around it largely ignores. Who needs it? We're trying to learn how to live.

What does this mean about Time? I briefly wonder.

Humans do rhythm, which is connected to a different kind of time than what this hapless device insists upon. We are not doing clock time; we are outside of it. The clock — and its mindless even-handedness — intervenes between the human body and its organic rhythms. Our hearts beat with varying speeds and intensities, and our breathing, though regular, is even less symmetrically configured. Possibly we humans would have been a less wretched collection of mutually exclusive and ungovernable passions if we had evolved a "clockwork organ" to keep us at least wobbling back and forth across the straight and narrow path to higher consciousness: but we did not. So, the clock ticks on, forever chopping each day into identical bits, while now and then, at unmeasured intervals, we catch the higher rhythm of someone (Natty Bumppo, maybe) out there in the gloaming, trying to walk silently upon a path of twigs and seeds.

The Pulse

If I did the exercise right, my soul would begin to merge with my entire diverse surroundings, and the edges of who I was would get increasingly blurred until my mind would jump and snap me back like a dog on a leash, scared of how far I might wander. . . . A current began to pulse between the mind of self-preservation and the mind of the natural instinct to become part of the life around me. After a year of practice, that pulse became so fast and habitual that it took on the character of a unique "third thing."

—Martín Prechtel, *Secrets of the Talking Jaguar*

WHY DOES THE CLOCK HAVE NO RHYTHM? Its purpose is regular, continuous, and trustworthy. Deftly it isolates and corrals unruly elements of the natural world into a smooth gesture that our attention span can happily recognize and relate to: the single thrust, followed by a short recovery, during which energy is garnered for another thrust. What a beautiful pattern to recognize and fall into! Over and over we are seduced by this regularity, and believe we have stumbled upon a basic and reliable template that sustains and provides an infrastructure, not only for entertainment, but for the fine arts.

We cherished this repetition pattern as children when we learned to follow the regular back and forth or up and down pulse of many songs and group activities. Giddy and engrossed, we fell easily into the contrast between being grounded and being aloft, as if these were the only and truly essential choices we would ever have to make throughout our entire lives.

Later we felt the one-two thrust-and-recovery pattern manifesting itself in a huge variety of other life activities: in building a house, in the pulse of orgasm, in snapping beans, in the countdown for a race to begin, in rocking a child to sleep, in how the baroque musician slightly ducks her head on each downbeat during a Bach gamba concerto. By thrust and recovery from thrust, we propel ourselves inexorably into the mysteries of life's higher rhythms.

Is this not what the clock is doing with its tick and tock? No, it is not. Its "beat" may be simple and compelling to imitate, but such imitation yields only a march, not a dance. The clock (particularly the digital clock) is conceived of and built to carry out its work without a short recovery between its thrusts. The clock is not making pulses that constantly quiver with the possibilities for slight variance; rather it is pounding equidistant stakes into the ocean of time. There is nothing to distinguish a "tick" from a "tock" except the words themselves. You might march to a clock, but you can't dance to it. The clock seeks to achieve all the benefits of rhythm by the one example of strict dual regularity; true rhythm is attached to the particular duality of our breathing.

When humans breathe normally, there is a definite break, almost a discontinuity between the inhale and the exhale. They hand off to one another: back and forth, forth and back they go, like a couple of marionettes gracefully tracing out a perpetual dance. But though they see-saw along as a unit called "breathing," they are not identical twins. For one thing, the human voice only works on the exhale, not on the inhale. We cannot emit a steady stream of sound, it must always be interrupted. And secondly, the pause at the bottom of the exhale is different from the one at the top of the inhale. There is a bit of a lurch at the bottom, the possibility of pausing a fraction of a second longer while the ambient air tide begins to flow unbidden into the nostrils, the mouth, the entire body. This inflow begins automatically, a second or more before the lungs actually start pulling. But there is time for a smidgen of conscious holding back (especially helpful for singers, divers, runners . . .) Every time, somewhere within the semi-conscious process of breathing, a little "silence" occurs, a place where the living body looks over the precipice and briefly faces the moment when the breathing stops. A nod only. And again at the top of the breath, a pause where the conscious and unconscious bump delicately into one another as the entire body rares back to make that turn like the cresting of a wave, before it releases the newly-filtered air back into the outflow, the flow of life. This is the mildly erratic rhythm pattern that is consistently available for the spoken word, and essential for poetry.

WHY RHYTHM AND NOT SOMETHING ELSE INSTEAD OR ALSO

so it came to me
to carry the abandoned
mattress to the attic

— Brian Teare

BELOW ARE THE OPENINGS OF SEVERAL POEMS. READ them quickly as you might while browsing in a bookstore or library. Ask yourself for each one, "Is this poem going to hold my attention more by the meaning and moral of the words — the story line — or more by the rhythms the words are making on their own as they clang and whisper and move together?

(1)
True story, Word of Honor:
Joseph Heller, an important and funny writer
now dead,
and I were at a party given by a billionaire
on Shelter Island.

(2)
I'm thinking of the boiling sea
and the dream in which
all the fish were singing.

(3)
And briefly stay, the junketing sparrows, briefly.

(4)
When Laurens van der Post one night
   in the Kalihari Desert told the Bushmen
      He couldn't hear the stars
Singing, they didn't believe him. They looked at him . . .

(5)
What a day it's been! What a thick milk light
compact, as if white-fingered, favors me!
I heard its red horse neighing
bare-backed, unshod and radiant.

(6)
This morning when I looked out the roof window
before dawn and a few stars were still caught
in the fragile weft of ebony night
I was overwhelmed.

The Rhythm of It

(7)
The wars are everywhere, o even within.
Drawn in poor bee by the dance loud hum
Of some other tribe, poor bee.
Even the center, even the heart,
Keeps a sting sharp: art stings thought,
thought stings art.

 This is not a test for which poems are better or worse, only an illustration of how the rhythms of certain poems can stimulate a subliminal "gut" response that immediately begins to override the "brain" information you are receiving from the narrative. As if your body is being seduced by a secret agent whose message is "Come with me, I will show you what's going on behind the scenes!" The poem seems to be feeding into you through two separate sources, one by sensibility into your brain, and the other by rhythm into your body. Except the same words are doing both. Such a "flowing into" way of receiving information seems to come by grace and is difficult to pin down, but merely being attentive to its possibility can enrich the reading experience far beyond what you might have been expecting.
 Rhyme can do this, as can a skillful laying on of numerically-guided metric frameworks. But I'm talking about an extended palette of rhythm patterns that are latent in normal speech, and only await the applying of a certain emotional intensity to bring them to the surface. These patterns are proportional and

asymmetrical, but regular enough to be recognized, repeated, and even classified. This is the poet's secret cache — like a shaman's bundle — as it always has been.

Rhythms like the ones found in the opening lines of poems 2, 3, 5, and 7 above are what pulled me into poetry when I was a teenager. Even buried in the tick-tock of song lyrics, I sometimes heard places where something had happened in the deliberate arranging of words that was not just an arithmetic balance adjustment to make the numbers come out even, but more like an alchemical transformation that essentially allowed words to be burnished and welded together so they could produce an entirely new meaning that they never could manage by simply trudging through various dictionary-sanctioned changes in context.

Since then I always begin reading a new poem by feeling forward into its rhythm, seeking proportional balance rather than repetitions. Do I start to sway in a dance that draws upon old patterns scratched onto my bones like petroglyphs? My stash of rhythm-incised stelae is large, and I have memorized them all joyfully. Finding one in a poem allows me to slip it on like a bridal gown, like a suit of armor, like a costume, like a new skin — a beautiful way of preparing to do full honor, once again, to poetry.

When this doesn't happen, I abandon my dance-seeking foray and switch to reading with my mind instead of my body. A good poem has many arrows in its quiver. I merely confess to a preference for being seduced by turning into a rag doll for a spell.

About Proportional Symmetry

Talking about proportional symmetry[2] in free verse poetry requires stepping aside from the traditional measuring terminology for metrical verse. A prosody is still involved, and numbers are also involved, but in the case of free verse, numbers offer only a clumsy translation of something coherently and precisely known through wordless experience; whereas in metrically-based prosody the poetic feet adhere to a system that privileges the numbers themselves over either the meaning or sound of the words.

Proportional symmetry shows up in the physical world spontaneously and continually. It's a set of simple, stable, harmonious relationship patterns within complex systems. These various basic symmetries can be represented as ratios of small whole numbers that look like fractions but are actually closer to prime numbers. The numbers that underpin these relationships are always even and odd, and they cannot be further reduced by division (i.e. 3/2, 4/3, 5/4). Because they are small and whole—thus integers—it would seem each of them could be "rounded up" and blended into a single digit instead of looking like loose ends from a finished product. These ratios are not static like fractions, but perpetually trembling on the brink of change, like the "unstable equilibrium" that sometimes briefly occurs between an immovable force and an irresistible object.

The fraction-resembling guise of proportional relationships, then, gives a false impression of yet one more system comfortably defined and sanctioned by numbers. We are accustomed to believing numbers are more exact than words. We rely on numbers—polls, surveys, statistics, stock market reports, price lists, bank accounts—to put the final stamp of value and truth on all complex human endeavors. When we fall back on mere words to talk about value in music and literature, we have the uneasy feeling that we've become sloppy or sentimental, abandoning truth and accuracy for the "comfort language" of the arts, which wallows in hugely abstract terms that are impossibly vague, imprecise, and therefore useless: *sweet, pure, harmonic, rhythmic, satisfying, relaxing,* and so on. If there is no overriding numerical confirmation, such words basically have no authority to give them purchase and may be released into the air like soap bubbles.

I am suggesting there is a compelling natural prosody embedded in language. Possibly in every language, but for our purposes, in English. This prosody is not regulated by numbers, nor on sets of stressed and unstressed syllables, but on various interweavings of the even and the odd. These two, of course, would not exist without one another, and yet when set forth as fractions—*parts* of a whole—rather than as entire, inseparable relationship units, the even and odd behave as if they have never heard of each other. They behave as if they have each stepped into our world from unique parallel universes to which they are loathe to return.

Once we let regular relationship patterns be split into separate numbers instead of leaving them in their original identity as proportional units, they started demanding the powers that numbers employ, and like characters in a fairy tale, they forgot that as soon as they climb down from the horse they came in on, they will suddenly collapse into dust. Yet we humans seem to have forgotten there ever was such a thing as recognizing and practicing proportional rhythm patterns in our poetry, with an accuracy based on "dem bones."

Proportional symmetry in the world outside poetry manifests itself visually as a pleasingly lopsided relationship among various whole units that naturally materialize in segments: flower petals, tree branches, the segmentation patterns of spider webs, the cracks in the mud at the bottom of a dry lake, the parts of the human body. Aurally and musically such symmetry comes forth as a scale system of individual notes that combine into intervals and chords that are either consonant or dissonant at the extremes, with an infinity of gradations between. I'm suggesting that free verse is and has been for centuries — millenia more likely — a spoken-word-generated poetry that keeps sending into the world new combinations of even and odd that are best recognized by our very own rhythm-wise bodies. The concept of proportion is innately non-arithmetical. Rhythm is molecular, organic, holistic, and simply lacking in the capacity to be numerically directed (i.e. counted) much beyond the number 10.

Next, let's look at proportional symmetry working in a poem.

Discovering a Proportional Rhythm in an Actual Poem

OPENING A BOOK OF FREE VERSE POEMS AT RANDOM, looking for proportional rhythms, I found this line:

Inside a metropolis of stars

Does this have proportional rhythm? My answer is yes. How does that rhythm go?

*IN-side
a me TROP o lis
of STARS*

In terms of small-whole-numbers there is a relationship here between 5 and 2, with the opening two syllables mirrored by the final two, and the middle five forming a kind of sub-symmetry with two unstressed syllables offering equal support on either side to a single stressed one, like a sip of water between cupped hands.

The whole phrase makes nine syllables, three stressed more strongly and six very lightly. In whatever way you combine the numbers, this pattern makes for a neat little proportional unit that probably could be found in many other free verse poems. To talk in terms of trochee, dactyl, and iamb here is irrelevant, because the "foot" or unit of conveyance is really the entire line. (And this remains true even if IN-side is heard as "in-SIDE," which it could easily be.)

As I looked further into this simple line, assuming it would serve as some sort of "proof" of the obvious gut strength of proportional rhythm, I discovered instead that the line was as full as a pincushion with other poetic indicators. Isolating this not terribly remarkable line—likely overlooked by readers on their way to the heart of the poem—strikes me as stark evidence that meaning and vocabulary also contribute to rhythm itself. Or, to put it another way, the image and idea in this opening stanza work together as a kind of chemical softening of the language-decoding part of the brain so that it can ingest several areas of "meaning" in a single flash. The comparison of starlight with the lights of a city, immediately locates the reader in a pivotal position of being in two places at the same time—earth and higher cosmos. This deft maneuver is accomplished through the elements of rhythm, music, image, and meaning, hereby enabling one another into a uniquely poetic way of knowing.

Please note a word of warning: if we want to be snarky, we can start counting stresses and syllables on everything. And lo! we have discovered proportional symmetry in prose. So what's "unique" about it? As an example, look at the prose statement in the third paragraph of this chapter: *Does this have rhythm? My answer is yes. How does the rhythm go?*

With some deft counting and arranging small whole numbers we could parse this into another unit of proportional rhythm, and who knows where that might lead? But the three short sentences would never get off the ground as a line of poetry. Why? Because as a line it has no imaginal heft. Its purpose is to convey information (or opinion) by the straightforward trudging technique: one foot after another, no trap doors, no leaps, no fireworks behind the eyes. The three sentences don't glom together as a poetic unit. Despite their resemblance to a proportional unit governed by small-whole numbers, they remain steadfastly sequential. Poetry is a thing made out of unintended consequences. A unicorn is not just a horse with a horn.

It takes a charged reciprocity between rhythm, music, evoked image, and meaning (or syntactical coherence, or rational thought) to meld a line into poetry. Poets have always walked the world with their ears extended like antennae, sifting the air for poetic snippets. They know the basic rhythms by heart, but need a constant supply of new images and ideas to pour into these rhythm patterns. For poets, spoken language has always been like a free mine — not as in "mine of information," but "mine of alternative meanings." The only catch is that poems have a mind of their own. Each time we try to marry a rhythm pattern to a set of words that seems to fit, the pattern is either smitten or not by the supplicants. If not, we can't look to meter or rhyme to bail us out; we have to put on our boots and go back out onto the land, like a bridegroom becoming worthy of his ideal bride.

The Walking of It

> Both the Inferno and, in particular, the Purgatorio glorify the human gait, the measure and rhythm of walking, the footstep and its form. The step, linked with breathing and saturated with thought, Dante understood as the beginning of prosody.
>
> —Osip Mandelstam, "Conversation about Dante"

I SELDOM WRITE A POEM WITHOUT HAVING WALKED through it first. That is, my body has a role as important as my brain in the process. My body's role is to discover and take into itself a rhythm that may be appropriate for an impending poem. The first part of the assignment—which like the Irish word *geas*, means, in this case, a personal quest that comes by way of holy decree, not a voluntary recreational activity—is to listen with my feet.

Walking through and then recognizing "an appropriate rhythm" means avoiding not only "inappropriate rhythms," but also ignoring or rejecting swarms of non-rhythmic motion patterns that might approximate rhythms but are not. Poetry simply cannot squeeze itself into a clump of narrative prose, no matter how grammatically correct or action-packed or poignant or even symmetrical it may be. Poetry rhythms ooze out of the ground as they have for as long as we can imagine, and the job of a poet is to regularly gather them up and match them with words. The process never grows old, because Earth, Air, Fire, and Water constantly roil into new patterns; or as Hopkins says, "new pangs, schooled by forepangs, wilder wring."

A poet's very first learning challenge is to figure out how to distinguish between a pattern and a non-pattern. After that comes "appropriate," and after that, the words. For poetry composition, the body is the first responder, way before the mind kicks in with its vocabulary.

All of this happens unconsciously — and by grace, not by checking off a list of instructions. A kind of sacred reciprocity[3] is involved, perhaps, but the universe has forever to overlook you, and that's just the rule. Your job is to hope that there may be an actual need for what you have to offer: another poem. And that you may be enlarged enough, once again, to make one happen. Just go out and take a walk, what could possibly go wrong?

As we walk, so we fall into our sparse infinity.

And, yes (for you literal ones, companions of my heart), I do "save up" walk rhythms somewhere in my fatty tissue, sinews, plasma, bones even. Many of them have likely been passed down for millenia, through one of those mysterious transmission processes unrelated to genetics — the way children learn from each other things their parents never taught them. In the case of poetry, the poetry rhythm stash is like the shaman's bundle, each one is unique and yet grounded in the same natural proportions that govern shape, structure, sound, color, texture as expressed in what we still call "nature," or "the natural world." The Platonic solids, golden section ratio, pi, strange attractors, the natural sine wave harmonics of the musical scale—these relationships are nature's architectural plans, expressed over and over, with abundance and austerity alike, and infusing everything that is. These structural analogies underlie and bring about the poetic rhythms that—I gently insist—remain available to the skilled poet like free ingredients for endless experiments that render them speechworthy. Like other poets down through the ages, I have simply re-discovered these rhythms by tracing them out with my feet. A kind of humming has begun: if I first get the rhythm right, I can hear the words before I know what they are.

Various anthropologists and others who probe deeply into the manifestly erratic nature of our species, *Homo sapiens*, have tried to choose a single, uniquely human behavior pattern that early on set us apart from other animals: spoken language; coded communications such as pictographs on the walls of ancient caves or various arrangements of stones into cairns; walking upright and the subsequent development of the hands; cooking; and then art itself, which like so many of our habits may have begun as a sort of idle ebullience but soon became an essential spiritual driving energy for our increasingly ambitious lives.

Whatever caused humans to become artists—potters, painters, dancers, singers, chanters, petroglyph carvers, jewelers, ritual tool makers, philosophers (yes, at some level I believe wisdom-seeking must be an art), and tellers of tales—we did not get there by engaging in mere survival activities, no matter how difficult or easy they were at any one place or time. We moved for moving's sake; we delighted in exercising our limbs. We developed into creatures for whom gyration is a language, a health regimen, a set of rituals, and a necessary precursor to almost any new behavior — bad, good, or otherwise. Walking/running is a thing we have ended up being extremely suited for. For humans, it is at once a *sine qua non* and *magnum opus*.

First is the stepping out, then the how of continuing to step, then the falling into the having-done even as you keep on doing, and the ultimate recurring meeting of the two (the starting and the continuing) in a kind of fission: This We Know.

In the womb we each swim and float in a dream of indolence. When we enter the world of air there is immediately a need for taking action to stay alive: to gasp, to kick, to squall. This pops us into a dimension we had not known before, where grieving our sudden enormous loss becomes our primary act as newborns, quickly balanced by a rude necessity to figure out how to substitute one kind of being alive for another.

At first not all our body parts seem useful, especially our little legs, still doubled up around our nether end like a couple of coiled springs. But after some months pass, they straighten, lengthen, and we finally discover a use for them, as we swing into the seemingly awkward and not terribly efficient stance that will remain our foundation and limit for the remainder of our lives. Feet at the bottom, head at the top, triangulates us. Upon this simple geometry we gain grace and agility as we learn and re-learn how not to topple. Our ridiculously small feet connect the whole of us to the ground, without which connection we would know far less than the slime mold. A better arrangement might have emerged instead, but it did not.

One of the by-products of walking upright on two slender sticklike organs, I believe, is poetry.

The instep, its bone geometries and the long drawn-out note of its downward slope. The do-overness of the walking, how it makes a constant lee for everything crossed by its shadow, thus thickening the floor of the world into soft pouches of relief.

Imagine poetry as a window into a world of early hominids who moved more slowly than their prey and could not swing through trees or bring their hands down to assist them in running. Walking took up an inordinate amount of time, and since they were stuck with it, they made an enormous variety of adjustments, including various hunting, hauling, and cooking tools. But walking was also a way of knowing. For the body was crawling along the ridgeline of the land the way a snake would do, feeling in every lump and crevasse a new way to flex; memorizing these ways; calling them up later around the fire to build together a communal stash, a larger world of stories and songs.

More Deeply into Proportional Rhythm

When you start reading a new poem, you're subconsciously expecting to be snagged by one of several primary poetry hooks. If none of these is present, your interest rapidly cools.

I'm calling these hooks rhythm, music, vision, and meaning. You could clarify this set of poetry hooks by attaching to them the senses that they tend to pleasure and stimulate:

rhythm — sense of balance and motion,
music — ears,
vision — eyes,
meaning — brain, mind, imagination.

These are the haptic pathways to the soul.

Another Example of Rhythm as a Hook

Below is the opening of a poem by Brenda Hillman, "Micro-minutes on Your Way to Work." The poem uses a simple form: each line has six words, and there are twenty-four lines. So immediately you have the tug and pull between lines and speech rhythms that you get in most free-verse poems. But in this case the tug is less influenced by syntax, or counted syllables, or accents. The six-word rule acts as a substitute for other reasons for line breaks and would seem to offer intriguing possibilities for rhythms, music and meaning to emerge.

> *Days are unusual. The owl sends*
> *out 5 zeros from the pines*
> *plus one small silver nothing. Where*
> *do they float? Maybe out to*
> *sea, where jellyfish are aging left*
> *and right. They have some nerve.*

The first three words announce themselves with a regular rhythm pattern of the dactyl: *Strong/weak/weak, Strong/weak/weak*. In music this is *One-two-three, One-two-three*. Just as you're getting settled into this easy three-by-six rhythm, the second three words, *The owl sends*, do a kind of hemiola[4] — another three-by-six rhythm, but one in which the weak beats are totally hidden beneath the weight of the three single-syllable words. Slightly off balance, you are gently debouched into an incantation of seven syllables: *out 5 zeros from the pines*.

Or, you could hear that as four trochees — Strong/weak — with the strong beats being Out, Zer, From, Pines. In any case, you have gone from a three-beat to a four-beat tempo, from odd to even — a downright cosmic shift.

The Rhythm of It

The next five words—"plus one small silver nothing"—thud rather prosaically onto the page, so that just as you're catching your breath from making the shift from one pattern to another, you're suddenly doing a little crawl in the gravel of prose, outside rhythm all together. Except for the "Where." This one word leaps into the breach and makes the syllables into an 8 pattern, so that the unaccented 7 syllables suddenly are knit together into an 8, and the balloon of rhythm lifts once more off the ground.

The "Where" now does double duty by latching itself onto the next set of words—"Where do they float? Maybe out to sea." This makes a beautiful 4/5 pattern of syllables and accents, and you can alter the accents slightly, according to what meaning you want to emphasize. In music, this would constitute a major third.

The ending of this section, "They have some nerve", echoes the other four-hammer-blow rhythms within this stanza: "Days are unusual" (sure, it could be spoken as six syllables but comes to the body as four, especially in retrospect); and "Where do they float?" Eagerly you read on into the poem, wondering if you will continue to be lulled by a meta-rhythm of 4-beat patterns, or be roused by yet another combination. As in music, you are tossed back and forth onto the petards of even and uneven small whole numbers—and their ticklish combinations.

Although this is a poem in which two other hooks, music and meaning (metaphor), play parts equal to the rhythm, I think it beautifully illustrates how a fine poet can sift through the unique rhythm offerings of several dimensions that would not normally coincide within the same thought-space, bring them unalloyed into this space, and fix them onto a word template that allows them to retain their original qualities even as they combine into something new.[5]

I see little point in imposing a number-based prosody for poems like this whose rhythms have already been distilled (or factored) by instinct, whim, and deep longing into the most efficiently possible way of delivering a multi-dimensional experience. What is at work is a clumping or clustering of phrases into (or, a splitting of phrases into) units of from one to ten words each, which retain the internal "intelligence" to arrange themselves in relationship with one another into patterns that the body viscerally responds to, both before and after the parsing brain is involved. This is a very, very old human passion, and one we should not treat lightly. It is a use of words distinct from that of prose.

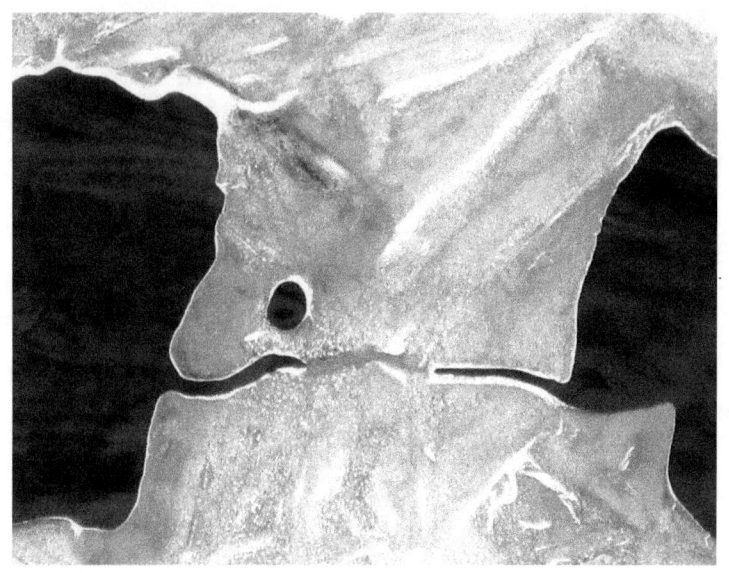

A Nod to Whim

Inequality in Baroque music is the rhythmically unequal performance of notes written equally.

— Robert Donington, musicologist

The whole of the day should not be daytime; there should be one hour, if no more, which the day did not bring forth.

— Henry David Thoreau

THE POINT OF THIS SMALL SET OF ESSAYS ON RHYTHM is not to suggest replacing a complicated and well-established system of poetic metrics with an equally complicated alternative. Rather it's the extension of a wistful analogy between verse prosody and the tuning of alternative temperaments on pianos. Having worked as both a piano tuner and a poet, I can't help but notice a similarity in the way numbers are rather casually wheeled in to provide an authoritative structure for a variety of conflicting, even mutually exclusive subsystems that are quite well taken care of by traditional artistic practices. With keyboard music you are confronted with a scale system that would like to ground itself in the physical laws of musical acoustics, with its ascending overtone series based on the natural divisions of a vibrating string (1/2, 1/3, 1/4, 1/5, 1/6, ad infinitum). But such a logical physics-sanctioned scale must deal with the inconvenience that each fundamental musical "string" produces an entirely unique set of overtones, and thus precipitates a continuous conflict between the tuned instrument (notes relatively fixed and few) and the music as a whole (notes many and all over the map). Where do these renegade notes come from? What natural system do they adhere to? Which piper are we following, anyway?

I sense a similar conflict when a poem is said to be, for example, in "iambic pentameter," yet there are instead half a dozen alternative ways the words could be spoken, none of which would come close to yielding anything so consistent or regular.

I realize we're temporarily combining pitch (musical scales) with rhythm (metrical beats) here, which might seem like comparing apples and oranges. But in each of these important facets of two separate arts, a conflict occurs because a huge set of distinct and recurring patterns asserts itself as regular enough to invite the "controlling" coding technique of number to catalog and regulate them — in essence to translate them — so that theory may blend with practice in a seamless art. At worst, what emerges in poetry is a metrical syntax that allow numbers to impose strictly timed intervals between words, even if this makes the meanings less clear. It's a little like opera, where you actually "get" what's going on in the plot much better when you don't know the meaning of the words.

The Rhythm of It

Rhythm is so central to both arts — music and poetry — that you would assume it to be reliably constant and clearly defined as a reference for how things are done.

However, numbers are really not much of a guide in either case. As soon as you pin an entire tradition beneath a set of metrical values, you run into what Thoreau was talking about above, a kind of "uncertainty principle" that usually remains conveniently hidden in the pages of musical compositions and poetry collections, but which becomes obvious in the heat of the moment — the actual performance.

As with language, the speaking comes first, and only later are the rules of grammar extracted from it. Language in that sense is like any art — it is not invented, it simply starts to happen, and continues to happen under its own organic set of relationships with the world. What we are confronting here at the deepest level is the relationship between "manifested" — completed, full and entire, unmoving, fixed — and "manifesting" — always in motion, always changing, never fixed. Such a relationship does and must exist, but it forges its own emerging pattern of coexistence. As poet Eugenio Montale said about poetry, "Compromise between sound and meaning does not admit of partial solutions in favor of the one or the other." He could have been talking about metrics and proportion.

You could also call it "being" and "doing." Here there is no compromise at all; the two must be yoked together inside a relationship of their own choosing.

In poetry this relationship between being and doing somewhat approximates a similar conflict between 1) a "traditional" prosody that identifies and validates rhythm by counting the patterns between strong and weak accents (feet) in each line of a poem; and 2) an even older, speech-based palette of characteristics that includes a gradation between strong and weak beats, a variety of pitch levels, lengths of syllable, and degrees of intensity. I believe this older system has never gone away and in fact continues to be evident in much contemporary poetry. I have no idea how conscious most poets are of its existence.

What I'm asserting is perhaps quite the opposite of T. S. Eliot's "ghost of meter" idea. Instead, the "ghost" I hear is that of certain spontaneous "plain speech" patterns that continue to emerge across the centuries as especially pleasing to the human body and ear, so that even when we hear them buried inside a complicated piece of prose, they ring out clearly and declare themselves (again) as candidates for promotion into a poem.

Here I must conclude by down-shifting into the rhythmic microcosm (maelstrom), the place where the pedal meets the metal, where systems shrug off their larger theoretical validations, and offer themselves to the full impact of raw experience. In this case, to be tempered by the ears, hearts, minds, and bones of the performers and listeners.

What composers/poets write down on the page, and what performers actually present, are often so drastically different that it becomes obvious that the rules are not only meant to be broken, but that a line is regularly crossed between constant and inconstant worlds. It is not a place you can even go with your mind, you simply must listen and feel your way in, moment by moment.

And yes, regard — for a second — the second as a convenient hinge between music's macrocosm and microcosm, between what is said to be happening and what is actually going on. Outside the second we can bask in the illusion of continuity and invariance: of order, justice, simplicity, comfort, prosperity, accuracy, love. Inside the second, however, the landscape darkens, sense loses itself. This is the country of ictus, chaos theory, unstable equilibrium, the uncertainty principle, notes inégal, rubato, strange attractors, fractals, the Higgs boson, the last visible dog, the surface of last scattering, and the problem of the variable dot!

It is the place-time ruled by the Law of Whim: anything that happens might just as easily have happened otherwise.

Listen here to an attempt by a scholar of medieval music to describe how rhythm is regulated in Gregorian chant:

> *The rhythmical ictus is simply a "dip" of the voice, an alighting place sought by the rhythm at intervals of every two or three notes in order to renew or sustain its flight until it reaches its final resting place. The ictus must be divorced from any idea of force or lengthening out. . . .*

If the ictus chances to be strong by its position, it does not appropriate the intensity thus bestowed upon it."

And a bit later,

The ictus is a mental division by the performer of beats of equal force into groups of two and / or three. Since, however, the ictus, while allegedly neither a stress, a shortening, nor a prolongation, is definitely perceptible, it is perhaps up to the physio-psychologist to settle the problem of determining what communicable form it takes.
— Gustave Reese, *Music in the Middle Ages*

This is a statement of music theory, based on performing and listening to Gregorian chant, but it comes across more like an existential meditation rather than a reliable guide. And note the absence of numerical terminology, of "measurement numbers" in that summary. Many who have listened to the various early religious chants will note how fluid and unpredictable they are in the "close" rhythmic alterations, as well as the subtlety of pitch changes, and especially how the music seems to blend with the architecture and materials of the surrounding building. A degree of close ear-listening is required by performers and audience, and the entire body of each listener is likely to be conscripted into the music as it flows around them. But after all these centuries, we still don't really know how it keeps on happening the way it does without losing its beauty, its continuity, its integrity.

The Rhythm of It

A fit analogy to the nature of musical and poetic rhythms is hard to pin down. New forms of poetry keep appearing as if by spontaneous generation. Yet old forms find ways to maintain their freshness, as do many forms of traditional music. This, I believe, is because the butterfly effect is not the same as unstable equilibrium is not the same as the uncertainty principle. "For the problem of the variable dot, though related to the problem of inequality, is not the same," said musicologist Robert Donington, who was waxing eloquent about the extremely restricted area inside which Baroque musicians were fully expected to ignore what was printed on the page. We take his point—subtleties matter when you are messing with the rules of the universe. In fact, the subtleties are the rules below a certain level. The tradition of poetry endures only because of the hidden, unpredictable parts, unpredictable not because our measuring instruments are not finely tuned enough, but because "measuring" no longer applies here. If there is consistency, we feel our way into it like bacteria, like flowers.

Perhaps humans can't truly influence either the microcosm or macrocosm, but we do seem to have access to a realm on the other side of sense into which we can take experimental lunges for the sake of poetry and music. Even the most rigidly rule-struck poet will occasionally wander over the line into the other side of the second hand on the clock and find herself inside kingdom of Whim, lost in the thronging dark.

RHYTHM REVISITED

> *We must give some examples of Dante's rhythms . . . Dante's poetry partakes of all the forms of energy known to modern science. Unity of light, sound and matter form its inner nature . . . In all seriousness, the question arises: how many shoe soles, how many oxhide soles, how many sandals did Alighieri wear out during the course of his poetic work, wandering the goat paths of Italy?*
>
> —Osip Mandelstam, "Conversation about Dante"

NOW I WOULD LIKE TO INVITE YOU INTO "THE INNER blindness of the compositional clot," to quote Mandelstam again. I've chosen a poem by Brigit Pegeen Kelly from her 1995 collection *Song* simply because the rhythm of the opening line has become an extra artery in my body. Here is the entire poem:

Of Ancient Origins and War

And briefly stay, the junketing sparrow, briefly,
Briefly, their flurries like small wine spills,

While the one divides into two: the heart and its shadow,
The world and its threat, the crow back of the sparrow.

Near the surface, beneath the soft penetrable mask —
The paste of white blossoms slurring the broken ground —
Alarm begins its troubled shoot: **the fruit tree**

Beareth its fruit: *a load of old fruit tricked out*
By the scattershot light, figured gold by the furious light.

The will given early to the dream of pleasure falters,
In a slurry of scent, in a posture of doubled-over gold,
And then there is the rift, the sound of cloth tearing

As the crow shoots up — fast with apparent purpose —
Splitting wide the leaves of a tree we cannot name,
Growing by a gate made from another tree, a gate

That cries as it swings, the cry of the broken safety.
The world and its haste, the world and its threat,
The here where we will die coming closer. All the sorrow

Of it, sparrow trouble, sparrow blow, our hands
These sparrows, quick and quick, but tippling now,

Toppling, bellies full of the bad seed the hair spilled
When it broke from the last comb it was locked into.
The will given early to the dream of pleasure falters.
And now, in the dark, listen, in the dark
The tulip poplar is singing, the leaves are singing,
The clear high green of a boy's imperilled soprano.

The moon is rising, the sound like wine spilling.
The boy will grow a beard, the boy will be bearded.
The bird will dive back down in perfect execution.

The damaged will can only watch and wonder
Through a surface alarmed with dust... And so now.
And so that now. We are in the trouble of a sleep

We did not dream of. And the shadows of the trees
Are breaking. The shadows of the world's broken vessels.

It's impossible to separate something called "rhythm" out of a richly-faceted poem like this. But let's think of rhythm as a lens — like infrared photography — that brings certain features temporarily to your attention as if they were the most important ones.

Reading through the poem strictly for sense, you realize it expresses a despair about the relentless inevitability of war in particular, but of wanton destruction more generally. The poem was written in 1995; but it could be about climate change or any of a number of present-day battles happening in the world, including on our city streets. Kelly makes her point metaphorically by setting up the fickle sparrows as examples of how we continue to chase after idle pleasure (junketing, wine spills) while our young men keep growing out of the hopeful dream of childhood into soldiers, and year after year push away the earth's continual offer of fruitful abundance, until now "we are in the trouble of a sleep we did not dream of."

For me the most prominent "rhythm" pattern is the

songlike repetition of certain words and lines. Her line repetitions do not fall into a standard prosodic form such as villanelle, sestina, or ghazal, but the line "The will given early to the dream of pleasure falters" rings out like a cymbal twice in the poem, as if sounding an alarm that has been reduced to the "tsk! tsk!" level of ignored parental advice, no longer able to rouse us from a state of fatuous and drugged indifference.

Beneath the clash of the cymbal she rings smaller alarm bells by cycling through certain words of small destruction: spills, divides, broken, alarm, furious, rift, tearing, splitting, trouble, execution, damaged — some of which she repeats. There are enough of these that the poem as a whole carries the power of an incantation — that is, the words and their meaning toll together as one unit, bypassing the brain and getting right back to our "fight or flight" instinct center.

Continuing with the incantation idea, the poem is almost alarmingly efficient in that most of the words, phrases, and single and enjambed lines work together through sound, rhythm, and meaning so that if you were watching the key words light up on a scoreboard each time they were used, you would probably be witnessing an equation for one of those strange-attractor symmetries. There is nothing random about her use of word and phrase repetition.

Her line rhythms tend to sound end-stopped even when they are not, because there is a dirge-like urgency to the poem, and that's how she achieves it. I find myself reading the poem as if each line were a full and final statement, so that I get the full benefit of

The Rhythm of It

the drama of this, while each time the line bleeds over into the next, I then feel myself quickly pulled into that secondary way of understanding.

This means I move through the poem slightly staggering.

There is a tremendous variation in the rhythm patterns she uses for her lines. Not to put too fine a point on it, the rhythms jerk you around like a rag doll on a stick. The opening line is divided into a 4-6-2 pattern. The first three words — And briefly stay — could be called iambic, with "brie" and "stay" being strong accents, "And" and "fly" being weak ones. But "Stay" invites you to linger a split second, making that syllable longer than the other three, and allowing for a small silence before you plunge into the pebbly mouthful of the next six syllables, basically unaccented. The final "briefly" is a small arrow into the heart; it stands there naked, half turned to look back at how it got here. Yes, it was all that junketing and not paying attention to the vital things. But let's have more wine, shall we?

If you let your rag-doll self float through the poem, scanning for "hits" of proportional rhythm, you may discover many small, piquant rhythm or meaning units that seem to have spontaneously joined forces and thus doubled their impact. This is similar to the way musicians move fluidly around among microtones in many ethnic traditions that deliberately utilize as many as twenty-two distinct pitches within a single scale. This is an organic poem in full health. It's all well and good to scan for iambic pentameter, trochees, or dactyls, but here you can also feel different parts of your body orchestrated to a fuller response.

Here are a few more rhythms that work their mysterious magic:

> *And now, in the dark, listen, in the dark*

This is a 2, 3, 2, 3 rhythm, like the perfect fifth in music, combined with the starkness of word repetition. As if your heart were a one-stringed instrument whom someone had just plucked.

> *The clear high green of a boy's imperilled soprano.*

Here you have two phrases, each with three strong accents but the first emerges as three hammer blows (given a little nudge by the opening "The"), and the second is also three strong accents, but they are buffered and lengthened by the intervening weaker accents, as if the whole line were a cable car trying to brake itself at the bottom of a steep hill.

Truthfully, there is hardly a line in this poem that does not slip into the body and find there a companion shape it can readily conform itself to. If the proportions of our bodies do not continue to have a role in producing poetry that qualifies as "The will given early to the dream of pleasure" then humans either never have, or no longer (as Hölderlin said) poetically dwell on this earth. I believe we do, and that our poetry must and does act in some way as a simulacrum of our core selves.

The Silence of It

*I am contented, for I know that Quiet
Wanders laughing and eating her wild heart
Among pigeons and bees. . . .*
  —William Butler Yeats, "In the Seven Woods"

POETRY, LIKE A UNICORN, SEEMS TO REQUIRE LOTS OF silence in order to show up.

Or is it *quiet* I mean instead of silence? The two words don't seem to be interchangeable. Isn't quiet like an inland lake, protected from the chaos of the open sea? Such lakes are dotted here and there, mostly hidden and rather rare—magic even. A state of mind is often involved.

Silence is unenclosable; it was here first, pretty much before anything else, and hasn't changed. It's not really something humans can experience, at least for very long. We (those of us who are not cosmological physicists) don't even have an inkling whether outer space is mostly noisy or mostly silent. Either, both, neither? We use the word "silence" to indicate absence of noise, which of course never really happens for any one of us while we are conscious.

Yet I would imagine we carry shards of Original

Silence (there is no other kind) around in our bodies as part of our construction formula (there being gobs of it available on Earth back in the day, and maybe it was handy to keep us from getting too dense). And while these shards are "parts" of the Original Silence, it is impossible for us to do more than tell ourselves the word over and over and define it — but we cannot find it or know it; silence is below our bottom line.

Leaving quiet out for the moment, let's bumble along as we started, with the relationship of silence to poetry. Let's say, "silence is to sound as poetry is to words."

Let's imagine that silence roams our world and sometimes inhabits a segment of space / time, effectively blotting out any sound that was there previously.

And as an analogy, poetry roams our world as an innately wordless being, which sometimes inhabits a group of words, effectively banishing any prior "narrative" meaning and instead infusing the words with an energy and meaning of their own. Poetry descends like the Archangel entering the soul of the Virgin Mary at the Annunciation.

Lack of sound may include silence, but does not completely define it, any more than a "poem" or "verse" (or set of formal devices) is a necessary condition for poetry.

So it's not silence that poetry requires in order to exist — rather, it's quiet, which perhaps in this case, following Yeats's example above, should be capitalized. Only by way of Quiet does poetry cross over from analogy (bound to narrative) to full metaphor. That would mean poetry doesn't need silence to exist, but it does need Quiet as a transforming place — a womb.

Thus, a person sitting on a bench in the sun overlooking a marsh can experience Quiet even with the distant uneven whisper of traffic, the shrill sound of children's voices, the passing whirr of bicycle wheels, and the constant soul-hammering knowledge of dwelling in a society enthralled by machines.

And continuing a bit further, even a person not on a quiet bench, but constantly exposed to noise of the most virulent sort (prison, explosives, brutal speech, automobile traffic, sirens, airplanes, or the hum of a generator at all hours of the day and night) can experience Quiet, too, if she can develop the right filters, discover entry into the right parallel universe.

If we divide poets, for a moment, into those who tend to develop their poems by drawing the universal "down" into the particular, or by injecting the particular into an assumed universal, then if this chapter were hoping to turn into a poem, I would seem to be starting with the universal. But in fact, this is not the case. The precise question of how quiet and silence are related and how they figure in poetry occurred to me in a particular place on a particular morning. I was out for a hike in the treeless public wetlands to the south of the town where I live, stopped to sit on a bench in the sun, closed my eyes, and became a happy vegetable. In a few minutes I shifted spontaneously — without any input from my brain and its words — into a dreamlike state of animal listening.

Inevitably my brain woke up, and hearing the

various noises, I realized to my delight that *at this very moment these sounds are not cancelling out the silence; I can still feel it around me!* And then continued: "How does this differ from true silence? It feels the same." And I realized that, yes, it did not differ at all in this particular time and place, even though there were plenty of sounds present. But then I quickly changed the word from "Silence" to "Quiet," because I knew Quiet had stopped by.

Quiet cannot be found on any map, enclosed refuge though it may be. "Where" is not part of its description.

Might silence be the raw element out of which Quiet can sometimes be spun? And if so how? And from what necessity?

WE SPIN

> *— the eye*
> *sees through the clock*
> *to the still within.*
> *No bone of previous.*
> *no shell of next.*
>
> — Greg Darms

A STORY IS TOLD OVER AND OVER.

A red, wiggly line appears on a cliff wall, wandering through the many fantastic figures of an ancient pictographic narrative. Some call it "serpent," some "water," it could be "entoptic visioning," "sine wave," "crenelated arch," or simply "path."

Whatever name humans give to this simple image is only the word part of an endless story. The sinuous painted shape is assumed to be "short for," "stand for," or "represent" something both inside and outside the human mind. But the wavy line might also be an independent entity, a kind of free radical in the world. What if it has neither a purpose nor a name? What if it kept presenting itself to the ancient painters, rising out of their bodies like spit, and then flowing through their fingers as part of whatever images they were making—as nature's persistent reminder of all that still remains silent and invisible on both sides of the wall?

The wavy line may be all that silence can ever do to reveal itself.

You can be swallowed by the serpent; you can slit open the beast, trace it, photograph it, revere it. You can drown in the water, drink it, bathe in it, follow its path. The silence will not contradict.

The ancient mythic images of rock art seem to be engaged in a process of their own, larger than the stories we tell about them. Yet they obviously belong in some way to us, since "we" made them, like a mystery revealing another facet of itself without the necessity of fulfillment. What might be our relationship with this particular—one of many—mysterious geometric shape laid atop our already geometrically expressed planetary geography? How may we translate the ubiquitous revealed presence of this curved line?

Might it be no more than the sine qua non it actually is, rather than what we later attempt to include it with? Might it be one of the universe's signals that we humans truly are, and are meant to be: fully alive? A sine wave is so basic that it need not be translated into a symbol for something else. Or, conversely, it's so basic we can use it as a symbol for almost anything.

But, again, what means this particular recurring visual sign, among many other recurring figures etched into or painted upon stone so well that the images — even above ground and subject to the weather — have endured for hundreds, even thousands of years?

What if we are confronting a kind of signature? The signature is fundamental and complete in itself; that is, not an acknowledgment of something much more complex and even more flexible. The wavy line is the human signing on to an understanding that the physical planet we live on is governed by sacred geometry, and as part of this planet, we agree to be joint signators of an enormous original contract, which mostly settles what our main contribution will be to the continued health of our dwelling place. This idea shows up in many mythologies in a variety of forms.

I am making a point here by attributing to a single "universal" symbol a heavy burden of meaning, but bear with me a bit longer. What if the wavy line is an actual, irreducible, untranslatable declaration of what we are here for? When "we" emerged from the welter of ancestral life paths into a fully modern and single hominid species, it turned out that our ticket into continued existence was that we spoke words as our language? Our chief uniqueness and therefore our chief value consists of our ability to spin silence into quiet, with our words. Our words, although quite useful for our own use, originally emerged to document the ongoing evolution of the world in which we are enmeshed. Our words are constantly spinning silence into quiet.

Raw silence funnels chthonically through all human lives, and pock-marks our endless yakettyyak. But what if all along the way it gets transformed continually into quiet? For some reason the universe needs this to happen. And though it is doubtful that we were specifically set down on the planet with this skill thumb-printed into our bodies, it came to be a thing that only we could do, albeit (for us, alas) not essential to survival.

There is really no analogy — it's simply that going directly from silence to words turned out to be too much of a jump for evolution to pull off. So, it doesn't actually ever occur. If there's a pause in our constant narrative, we assume there is mumbling going on in the background; we just can't hear it.

Nature works through a coagulation of contingent redundancies. There is a famishing generosity in this.

Our contribution to the "redundancy" part (think blossoms falling from trees; think how many eggs an octopus produces compared to how many little octopi survive into adulthood; think swarms, think seeds, think sunsets . . .) is our endless repetitions of the same phrases through time. We may be building a new universe after all.

Thus the stories we tell, the individual persons we grow into, pass through, and shed do not slip to the ground like dead leaves, even though we repeat ourselves. It simply takes a long time to make quiet. If this peculiar spinning is a task, and one that can be completed — or will at least accumulate obvious heaps — then there should come a moment when the ratio of silence-to-quiet has tilted far enough so that some other way of being can begin to emerge and robustly cavort in our universe. Perhaps when that happens, we will all re-awaken and know ourselves anew.

Smuggling the Poem Across

FROM THE READER'S POINT OF VIEW, SOME POEMS seem to bypass words. The whole poem has made it across that mysterious bridge from the wordless into the narrative realm, naked and holding its original weight. It is carried from the place where it emerges like a worm in the heart, and where it has grown into a serpent ready to eat you alive unless you get rid of it. The poem is smuggled across the gap before it wakes up the border guards, who would make telling demands on it: they would require that the poem be told. The serpent-about-to-become-poem is coerced into keeping quiet on the bridge because, knowing nothing of words, it believes it is about to be tolled — a far better fate.

Certain poems actually say something quite different from what they seem to say. Nobody is responsible. You look up from your chair in the middle of the night and see that it has been transported out into the front yard: there you are in your pajamas with your glasses crooked on your face, looking surprised and angelic among the moon-dark maple leaves. A sort of spontaneous generation has occurred, creating a Third Thing that has no true origin, that cannot be predicted, traced or duplicated, only dumbfoundedly enjoyed.

All good poetry does this to some degree; there is a mist, an aura that rises from the poem and is taken in like a perfume to enrich its overall effect, or to give it ambiguity and (at least) a double meaning. But in rare instances a poem even travels beyond its usual ration of metaphor and reveals that it has transcended the fractal boundaries of a single infinity — in a parade example of "having a mind of its own."

Such a poem is twice-told and thrice received, like a minor god(ess). That is, between the wordless but vitally-charged raw energy that gathers in the creative cauldron of the poet's heart and the final set of careful, mind-vetted words that give this material heft, shape, and meaning as a legitimate piece of language art rises a Third Thing like vapor from an alchemical experiment. It is this Third Thing that turns out to be the poem.

Such poems, like landrace species that appear randomly amidst rows of genetically predictable grains, or like the ungainly swan showing up in a bevy of fluffy baby ducks, can sometimes appear like a small miracle to both poets and their readers. But can we do this on purpose?

Poetic Logic

ONE OF THE WAYS POETRY DIFFERS FROM PROSE IS that poetry makes "leaps." At least that's one explanation of why poets don't always write in complete sentences. After all, people don't dream in complete sentences, nor when we're awake do we think first and speak afterwords with a decent interval between. Words are ever only a vague approximation of what the whole self is actually going through at any given time. Poetry is a use of words that permits especially large gaps between words and meaning.

But even poets have their leaping limits. So, I want to illustrate an example of what I think is poor poetic leaping. It's a very small poem to beat up on, and yet the poem threw me into a small dilemma, for reasons that I outline in my response to its author.

This poem was mailed to me shortly after the tragic and sudden death of a mutual friend. The poet could not be present at the memorial, and asked — if the opportunity arose — if I would read this poem aloud on his behalf. I agreed to do so before having seen the poem, and as it turned out, there was no opportunity. When I returned home I wrote the following letter to the poet (I include the poem first):

*A leaf falls
and we all
are less.*

Dear X,

Your poem arrived today. Being the philosophical scamp I am, I have been unable to quiet the questions it raises for me.

 Aren't leaves supposed to fall? Even if we make ourselves small enough to mourn a leaf (since people are supposed to die, too, but we feel sad about that and don't feel sad about leaves because we're the wrong size for them) — even then, doesn't the supposed-to-fall of leaves fundamentally differ from that of people?

 Different leaves come back, but in a sense they are the "same" leaf, aren't they?

 Different people come back, but we don't think of them as replacements of the ones who died.

 Are we actually "less" because a leaf falls? This is a terrifying thought. "We," meaning the entire world of humans. It could be true, although it would signify an appalling abundance to be so continuously reduced and for so much to remain. Besides, if you apply the vegetation analogy, then every time a leaf grows out we must be "the more." Therefore, if loss is balanced by renewal (in the matter of *leaves)*, how can we become "less" whenever a single leaf falls?

I guess I'm saying I don't believe the assertion in your poem — meaning: it is not my philosophy, not meaning: you were speaking falsely.

I think we silly humans are made of moons, and each of our moon systems is in a complex of phases. My moons simply don't allow me to believe that I am less because a leaf falls, and neither are my kin. Quite the contrary. But if I were sitting on the porch, as you were, grieving over the loss of our friend and possessed of your particular moon system, I might understand. Is there a way your poem could be expanded to overcome that saucy moon of mine that sticks out too far?

– Anita

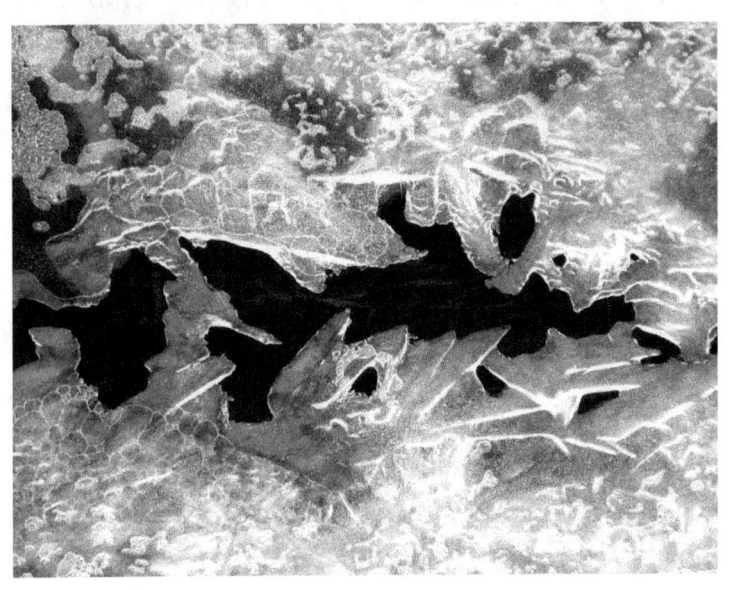

Speech Rhythm as Perpetual Mystery — I

An extremely basic example of how speech and rhythm work together might be, simply, counting. Counting aloud from one to ten is not quite gibberish, but it's not real talk either: each number is a one-syllable word (except for "seven"), but they don't combine into phrases or sentences, they only make a string of sounds. You have to listen especially hard to catch any tendency towards rhythm.

Nonetheless, reciting the numbers from one to ten is not the same as saying the same word ten times. You can hear the potential for speech rhythm even in this bare-bones list. Each number-sound is different from the rest, requiring a different movement of your lips and tongue, the speed and force with which you release the air, the sense of restraint or freedom each syllable requires for clarity, so that you adjust your voice and mouth as if you were blowing them out as bubbles to set gently on a shelf. And you may feel the whole string of words flowing into each other like a song of syllables, the way you are taught the alphabet. But unlike saying the alphabet, for example, each number is also a word with its own history, just like "house" or "ghastly" or "collide." Any word, when given voice, will rub across the individual memory of the speaker and make a tiny quiver in that enormous web, a shaped quiver that is composed of every experience this word has taken part in during that person's life.

This is the potential power that words hold as their heritage.

The human body is a contained space like a kaleidoscope inside of which an enormous mosaic of rhythms act out their constantly shifting motion patterns every minute of every day for you to react to: infinite patterns within a finite space. Yet while there may be a million distinct pattern combinations for the million distinct voiced sounds we are capable of hearing, there are actually not very many we can distinguish enough to name, repeat, and combine into music or language. The result is an enormous nesting of smaller "almosts" within larger absolutes. The clock, you might say, is merely a smaller absolute with nothing inside to contaminate it into beauty.

Poetry is one of the distinguishing tools. It "catches" certain patterns in its net, patterns that conform to the geometry of proportions on which all natural structures are based. These patterns express themselves in musical acoustics as pure musical intervals; in the atomic and molecular structures of biology and physics, and in geology, architecture, and geography as proportional relationships such as golden section, *pi*, and a host of triangulations among natural and constructed phenomena around the globe. The more

The Rhythm of It

you refine your listening skills, the more of these fundamental proportional rhythmic combinations you will learn both to "feel" in your bones and to recognize when they occur in spoken language, and to respond to intuitively. Poetry polishes and reinforces these responses by a kind of sand-castle tactic: adding more sand here, taking more away. Not randomly (that would be mudpies!) but subtly and subversively by pleaching each poet's individual internal geography onto the basic phylogeny and ontogeny of our thus-far-realized nature as physical organisms governed by the same laws that allow the natural dance of life. Poetry is that pristine.

Poetry is not song lyrics, but it's not ordinary speech either. I'm jumping onto the poetry merry-go-round at the point of entry called "rhythm," as if that were somehow the True Beginning place. But many fine poems prioritize something other than rhythm. Is that even possible? I ask myself. Surely I am just not listening deeply enough. For me, if a poem fails the secret test: Does this make my insides dance? I am at a loss to fit the poem into my wrought system. Nevertheless my shelf includes a pile of poets whose work I confess myself seduced by for some other reason than listening with my feet. This keeps me from becoming smug and believing I have set up a System That Includes Everything.

Some sort of amazing dispensation has once again comported itself, re-defining grace. Poetry redounds to the elemental, again and always, complete in itself, not a chemical compound acting out $1 + 1 = 2$, but bringing forth yet another 1.

Speech Rhythm as Perpetual Mystery – II

The tongues of mocking wenches are as keen
As is the razor's edge invisible,
Cutting a smaller hair than may be seen,
Above the sense of sense. . ."
　　　　—William Shakespeare, *Love's Labors Lost*

BECAUSE I DO NOT WANT THESE MUSINGS TO TURN into a work of literary criticism, I have avoided lengthy examples of various proportional–rhythm patterns that I am claiming as underlying much contemporary—especially so-called free verse—poetry. I have not devised a prosody "system" to describe these rhythms because it would have to include too much—like a map of the earth as big as the earth. It would include degrees of accent, rather than simply strong and weak; it would include quantity, or varying lengths of syllables (quantitative meter, which English is supposed to lack); pitch; emphasis; and most elusive of all, a set of body-responses to the general lilt and shape of the various rhythm patterns, some of which have become sufficiently formalized to be described, nonetheless depend upon a kind of fractal freedom (infinity within finite boundaries) to remain alive and able to keep generating new "prime" versions of themselves.

Where do lines of poetry come from? How in the world does anyone think up those word-spurts that sort of make sense, but not in the usual way of conversation? Nobody would ever be able to talk this way, even if they wanted to. It's too unique. Like the Shakespeare quote above, it's "above the sense of sense." It's also too precise.

Again, how does poetry resemble normal talk? When we are talking directly with other people, the words seem to come out before we've even thought them up, essentially bypassing the brain. The process is not like this: first we think what we want to say; next we translate the rough thought into a full sentence; then we say it. That would be way too slow, like a cow chewing its cud.

One possible reason we can speak faster than we think is that most conversations are simply re-runs of previous ones, going back and back through time. We talk in cliches that we can churn out in our sleep. It's as if we all carry around a generic recording in our minds of phrases that can be rapidly assembled out of the vocabulary most recently used and therefore still "in the system." If the conversation gets a bit more philosophical or information-heavy, and we venture into new territory where we have to stop and dive more deeply for information or careful opinion, we might try out an entire phrase in our heads before we actually repeat it aloud. But even then, conversation happens like a net game, you have to be ready to hit the ball back as soon as it appears again. You have to think with something quicker than your brain — something that stores pre-combined thought-and-word packages.

Poetry, although nowadays generally first written rather than spoken — and therefore born into the world already once-removed from normal talk — also combines thought and word in a way that does not follow a logical sequence. Image / idea / thought / word all seem to bunch together, fueled by some kind of special — I would even say "local" — passion that rises for the occasion. But for poetry, I believe "something else" needs to happen to propel the poem into existence. I call it a third thing, even though it's not a "thing," but more of a context or a knot of necessary distractions that have nothing to do with the poem at all, but present like the occasion for sin.

This is not a neat process. A poem often unfolds into a state of unstable equilibrium, like a clock pendulum upside down; it can remain in precarious balance only by constant assistance from an outside force, a third thing. Each poem, as it passes through its creation process, may be offered, gratuitously, at least one rhythm pattern that functions like a new prime number. If the poem "chooses" to take on this pattern, anomalous, yet wholly appropriate, it may avoid being flipped back over into a more docile and less interesting stability where most poems remain. Like being offered a short and glorious life, or a long and prosperous one out of all public view.

For such a poem to come into existence, something else has to happen, which you, the poet, have no control over, but which would not be happening without you, will not finish happening unless a poem results from it, but that needs to happen in some sense before the poem begins. This means you, the poet, may find yourself in the unstable position of engineering an event that you deeply long for and cherish, are responsible for and participate in, yet you do not have in your hands a plan for. You must do this over and over. You don't know the outcome, and you're not sure exactly what you are doing, therefore you are doomed never to be able to replicate the process because the process itself is part of the outcome.

It's as if the outcome, a finished poem, were dreamed in advance by something other than you, and you are going backwards through the process. *And this is the process.*

POETRY AND RITUAL

THE PROCESS OF COMPOSING A POEM BEGINS WITH AN experience. The poet must enact a poem before she can write it. This means no poem will be the direct documentation of an experience; rather it will be the documentation of a ritual.

The ritual is a kind of transference mechanism to get from the wordless realm of felt image, thought, and impression to the finished poem, so that the poem will embody something essential that is otherwise isolated by being inexpressible. This ritual is a bridge between realities, a bridge that language itself can neither do first nor alone, but only by following the ghostly prints left by direct action.

The order goes something like this:
- trigger experience;
- recognition that a poem may emerge from this experience; and
- a pause to choose and activate a personal code — words, gestures, images, mnemonic devices, sounds — that are meant to take you back just prior to the trigger experience so you can enact it rather than simply remember it.

When you begin to assemble the poem, which is, at best, only a series of hints and not a direct telling of anything, there is a pretty good chance you may not find the experience again in the same raw form. This is especially the case if you have, in another part of your brain, been prematurely fiddling the direct experience into words, into a told state, and thus bypassing the ritual. Rather than being some kind of filter or intermediary meant to refine or shape the experience into a poem as opposed to some lesser form of telling, the ritual includes the poem and the original experience together; the ritual simply shows up when the original experience is powerful enough to attract it.

Therefore, each time you first "tell" a poem into existence, it must be as a recounting of a ritual, not of the experience itself. The ritual honors the triggering experience, but is not meant to convey it directly; rather the ritual is meant to bypass the narrative and go directly to the kind of transference that only poetry can pull off.

You perform the original ritual within the normal set of converging shapes that daily orbit and suffuse your soul. Some of them are totally new, some are old and familiar, like the stage sets for a play that you keep moving around into different configurations, re-painting, re-draping with new cloths.

The poem cannot emerge wholly until and unless your soul completes its ritual of assimilation. This honors the value and weight of the initial experience, granting it a kind of passport to make the final journey across the border into the realm of words — where it has never been.

Plain Speech

I BELIEVE, ALTHOUGH I DO NOT KNOW, THAT POETRY has remained useful and necessary as long as humans have been able to speak, and that its usefulness and its necessity depend on there being a distinction between poetry and ordinary speech. Nothing equal about this distinction; it usually pushes poetry over to a peg on the wall, where it hangs like a school fire extinguisher with its sign: Do Not Break Glass Except in Case of Fire. This is because poetry is innately formal and rhetorical, and it takes a special effort to hang out in that space. Poetry is a deliberate use of language for some purpose that includes emotional arousal. Poetry is a wielded thing. It might not actually start fires, but it certainly does not extinguish them.

How do we tell them apart, then, once we've absolved poetry from rhyme and meter? It must be something about the vocabulary! Poetry and plain speech share free access to everything in the dictionary. There is no ancient, secret "poetry only" vocabulary bundle that poets carry in a little leather bag around their necks. And unlike the hundreds of balkanized vocabularies used in politics, sports, economics, law, medicine, etc., neither has poetry insisted upon its very own definitions for many common words. Nonetheless, certain words seem to take on a special glow when they inhabit a poem: moon, glass, star, silky, light-filled — as if a poem were a room, almost a chapel, inside which normal words are charged with extra meaning just by being there.

Yes, it is partly vocabulary that gives poetry its almost visceral power. But I insist that this happens because poetry is analogous less to plain speech and more to scientific or legal language, in that it is extraordinarily precise in its quest for truth and accuracy. Nevertheless, the only way the poet can adequately polish her poem into a wielded thing is to temporarily, but repeatedly, leave vocabulary altogether and dive for the metaphor — always lurking beneath anything said — as its wordless origin.

I have tried to make the distinction between poetry and prose primarily dependent on rhythm, partly because I don't believe vocabulary is enough to explain the impact that a fine poem can have on a listener/reader, but mainly because it's the poets who have always been able to "hear" the many well-proportioned rhythms in plain speech and extract them for their poems. If readers and listeners still can't tell any difference, they are simply missing out on a whole dimension of literary art.

But there is another distinction between poetry and plain speech that I do not have an explanation for and can only give an example of. Even if a poem fails the test question: "Can it be written out in prose form and not sound weird?" by answering "Yes," this

The Rhythm of It

does not inevitably condemn it to be relabeled as a short story or essay or conversation. For some reason you've hit bedrock. The alembic has reduced the ingredients into a single element, which cannot be further distilled.

Hence, this chapter, where I'd like to touch upon a favorite poem that almost totally lacks the wonderful proportional rhythm patterns that always cast a spell upon my body before I've even registered any sense to the narrative. This poem could be written in paragraph form, as a story. But it is a poem.

First, to remind ourselves of the contrast we're exploring, here's the first stanza of a poem that does "got rhythm," and its rhythm immediately opens the small purple door in the back of the enormous yew tree with the dark, twisted trunk. You enter quickly, before the narrative part of your brain lights up and starts demanding a plot.

*Say despite all the churches with their unlocked doors
and outstretched strangers' palmskin, I hungered still*

When I *read* (that's past tense, rhyming with "red") these lines for the first time one morning on my computer, I immediately thought "Oh! one of those!" and eagerly continued. Why?

Because you are immediately released from one way of knowing into another. The words don't make the usual kind of sense. In the back of your soul some gears crunch a little as you shift into an atypical way of receiving information from language.

You are released into a place where the sound and rhythm convey as much as the narrative, and you have to receive through other parts of your body than your brain.

Because, more specifically, there is a kind of rhythmic funnel that rushes and swishes you down a spillway into the final three words: "I hungered still." Along the way you are struck like a gong by the rhythms of magic and pathos: "unlocked door," "outstretched strangers' palmskin." You become dimly (or maybe intensely) aware that the meanings of the words form part of the rhythm, part of the music. The word-and-rhythm pattern of this opening allows entrance to a place where meaning can subtly and mysteriously come at you from a dozen or so dimensions.

Also, because the rhythm is vaguely close enough to ten syllables a line to give you a sense of traditional English poetry's iambic-pentameter comfort zone, even though it is not that at all. We can't help that our rather slothful bones insist on defaulting to that meter, as if it were the only deep incantation we need remember or endure.

Now let us turn to a poem that seems to pay no attention to a distinction between "poetic" rhythm and just plain prose. Yet it gets past my defenses, and for me, still qualifies as poetry.

The three-page poem by Larry Levis, "Elegy with a Bridle in Its Hand" documents an epiphany by expressing the author's full presence at the moment he sees two old horses he has known for many years.

The Rhythm of It

> *One was a bay cowhorse from Piedra and the*
> *   other was a washed-out palomino*
> *And both stood at the rail of the corral*
> *   and both went on aging*
> *In each effortless tail swish, the flies rising, then*
> *   congregating again*
> *Around their eyes and muzzles and withers.*

In terms of rhythm, this is prose. It could be set as a paragraph. It sounds a bit like the opening of a novel.

So what hooks me about it and strongly hints that this will be a poem and not just another example of lineated prose, is the phrase: "and both went on aging."

Levis almost stops time with this phrase, but not quite. Suddenly he "sees" these two old horses as a kind of blur, as if he had entered a molecular level of reality and was actually able to catch them changing each nano-second into their final physical selves, a heap of unfleshed bone dust.

The poem is about two old horses he is observing, and also about how his remembering of them fondly is as worthless as the horses themselves were always seen to be:

> *They were worthless. They were the motionless*
> *   dusk and the motionless*
> *Moonlight, and in the moonlight they were other*
> *   worlds. Worlds uninhabited*
> *And without visitors.*

The poem gains momentum very gently and powerfully as he finds himself both seeing the world—even the entire universe—through the temporary clarity of his attention to the particular trajectory of these two old horses. As if there could be a "particular trajectory" to something so relentlessly generic.

> ...for a while I began to think that the world
> Rested on a limitless ossuary of horses where their
>   bones and skulls stretched
> And fused until only the skeleton of one enormous
>   horse underlay
> The smoke of cities and the cold branches of trees
>   and the distant
> Whine of traffic on the interstate.

Somehow, in his arhythmic lines—without resorting to a Biblical or solemn epic storytelling kind of rhetoric—Levis saunters through a rueful but extraordinarily tender realization that two worthless horses and a human observing them comprise a moment that will not contribute a single grain of meaning to the future of the universe. Yet this is the moment he would choose above all others to hold as his own. He accords to this moment the full skill of his wry metaphorical heart, as if the sheer love of these two ancient equine nonentities pulls out of him a level of singing even he would not normally endure:

wordless and tuneless preoccupation involved them

The Rhythm of It

The horses cannot and also have no wish to speak for themselves; therefore, nonetheless, anyhow—he, Levis, will do them the honor for no particular reason. An almost holy diffidence rises out of the poem.

The rhythm, if that word still must be catered to, seems to come from a kind of tectonic powering-through of the poet's raw necessity to reach a certain deep understanding that words are normally unable to pull off, but that writing the poem is nonetheless the only way that this experience will have occurred at all.

Like Levis with his worthless moment, I have to conclude there are no pre-conditions for poetry; each poem is an emergent property that in its creation either does or does not "emerge." If there is a cause at work here, its name is whim. A similar conclusion from two medieval Arabic philosophers will close my book:

> *He asked me this question: "What manner of solution have you found through divine illumination and inspiration? Is it identical with that which we obtain from speculative reflection?" I replied: "Yes and no. Between the yes and the no, spirits take their flight from their matter, and heads are separated from their bodies."*
>
> —Ibn 'Arabi upon meeting Averroës, twelfth century

Conclusion

> . . . *generations have trod, have trod, have trod*
> — Gerard Manley Hopkins

ALTHOUGH IT USES THE SAME WORDS, POETRY operates within a parallel dimension from that of prose. Poetry sifts, funnels, and amplifies the sound and rhythm facets of vocabulary in a way that, when triangulated with meaning, ultimately provides humans with a sixth sense. This secondary and almost transcendent ability of poetry to tread the same circuits of hearing, seeing, and touch used by the prose of conversation and informational discourse, while parleying the raw material of words and meanings into what amounts to a bodily organ of perception, can allow access to higher levels of consciousness.

A poet well schooled in a contemporary version of the ancient art of poetry will be able to walk the secret pathways that access this dimension. Or, unschooled but ardent, she may discover these pathways herself. And so long as there remains an audience who cares enough to notice whether or not some of the poems they read or poets they listen to have transported them body, mind, heart, and soul into this dimension, then poetry can continue to carry out its particular version of the original assignment: assuring the existence of the Beauty that keeps the world alive.

NOTES

ENDNOTES

1   "Aksara" means syllable, but in a huge, metaphorical sense.

2   A more complete discussion of numbers and proportions in the Western musical scale may be found in my book *The Seventh Dragon: The Riddle of Equal Temperament*.

3   Sacred reciprocity is one of the twelve (or so) core principles or sacred values embodied in shamanic traditions. It holds that generosity is an endemic energy held and cherished by nature; therefore, living generously is an essential lifelong practice for true health and wisdom.

4   In music, hemiola refers to a shift in emphasis within the time signature; the original time signature is still followed, but the feel of the rhythm seems to switch into a totally different pattern. As when you are in a six-pattern that goes *ONE/two, ONE/two, ONE/two* (3 times) and suddenly switches to *ONE/two/three, ONE/two/three* (two times).

5   This may be an example of what Thomas Aquinas called the problem of "Mixed Bodies." The question is: when strongly defined elements (chemically, physically, philosophically) come together in a larger system, how do they "blend"? Do some of them dissolve their original boundaries and essential qualities in order to accommodate a new whole, or is it possible for each to retain its defining behaviors and powers while at the same time contributing to a new whole they were previously not associated with. So far as I can understand, the "answer" is sometimes this, sometimes that — allowing for an uneasy coexistence between two possibilities that should not be able to become actual at the same time and place.

Poetry References

page 23 (epigraph): Brian Teare, "Separation is the necessary condition for light," *Poem-a-Day*, Academy of American Poets, October 22, 2013.

page 23 (1): Kurt Vonnegut, "Enough: The Joe Heller Poem," *The New Yorker*, September 2, 2013.

page 24 (2): Paul Guest, "Post-Factual Love Poem," *Poem-a-Day*, Academy of American Poets, June 30, 2017.

page 24 (3): Brigit Pegeen Kelly, "Of Ancient Origins and War," *Song* (Rochester, New York: BOA Editions, 1995).

page 24 (4): David Wagoner, "The Silence of the Stars" *Traveling Light: Collected and New Poems*. (University of Illinois Press, 1999).

page 24 (5): Pablo Neruda, "Dream Horses," translated by Nathaniel Tarn, *Pablo Neruda: Selected Poems* (Boston: Houghton Mifflin, 1990).

page 24 (6): Joy Harjo, "Song for the Deer and Myself to Return On," in *Mad Love and War* (Middletown, Connecticut: Wesleyan University Press, 1990).

page 25 (7): Dan Beachy-Quick, "Song," *Poem-a-Day*, Academy of American Poets, August. 25, 2014.

page 33: Quinton Hallett, "When Demons Blink," in *Mrs. Schrödinger's Breast* (Eugene, Oregon: Uttered Chaos, 2015).

page 101: Jerika Marchan, "A Crumb in the Cobblestone — Tell Me This Landscape Darkened Without You," *Poem-a-Day*, Academy of American Poets, June 14, 2018.

Bibliography

The following is a partial list of sources either directly used in the book or that, over time, strongly influenced the ideas presented here. I am omitting countless essays, which would have extended the list for several more pages (and would have rectified the dominance of male authors in this list.)

Calasso, Roberto. "Meters are the Cattle of the Gods." In *Literature and the Gods*. New York: Alfred A. Knopf, 2001.

Jorgensen, Owen H. *Tuning*. East Lansing: Michigan State University Press, 1991.

Lawlor, Robert Lawlor. *Sacred Geometry*. London: Thames and Hudson, 1982.

Mandelstam, Osip. "Conversation About Dante." In *Mandelstam: The Complete Critical Prose and Letters*. Ann Arbor: Ardis, 1979.

Menocal, María Rosa. *Shards of Love: Exile and the Origins of the Lyric*. Durham, North Carolina: Duke University Press Books, 1993.

Perloff, Marjorie. "After Free Verse: The New Nonlinear Poetries." In *Close Listening: Poetry and the Performed Word*. Edited by Charles Bernstein. New York: Oxford University Press, 1998.

Prechtel, Martín. *Secrets of the Talking Jaguar.* New York: Tarcher/Putnam, 1999.

Reese, Gustave. *Music in the Middle Ages.* New York: W. W. Norton & Company, 1940.

Steiner, George. *After Babel: Aspects of Language and Translation.* Oxford: Oxford University Press, 1998.

Tomlinson, Gary. *Music in Renaissance Magic.* Chicago: The University of Chicago Press, 1993.

Veyne, Paul. *Did the Greeks Believe in Their Myths?: An Essay on the Constitutive Imagination.* Translated by Paula Wissing. Chicago: University of Chicago Press, 1988.

Winn, James Anderson. *Unsuspected Eloquence: A History of the Relations between Poetry and Music.* New Haven: Yale University Press, 1981.

About the Author

Born under the sign of Libra, Anita Sullivan cheerfully admits to a life governed by issues of balance and harmony. This likely led to her career as a piano tuner, as well as her love of birds (Libra is an air sign), gardening, music, and fine literature. She spent years trying to decide if she was a piano tuner who wrote poetry or a poet who tuned pianos. She traveled a lot without becoming a nomad; taught without becoming a teacher; danced without becoming a dancer; fell totally in love with the high desert country of the Southwest and promptly moved to the Pacific Northwest rainforest. She has previously published two essay collections, a novel, two poetry chapbooks, and a full-length poetry collection. Her collection of short essays, *The Bird That Swallowed the Music Box*, was published by Shanti Arts in 2018. She was a founding member of the Portland, Oregon, poetry publishing collective Airlie Press.
• www.anitasullivan.org

SHANTI ARTS

NATURE ▪ ART ▪ SPIRIT

Please visit us on online
to browse our entire book catalog,
including poetry collections and fiction,
books on travel, nature, healing, art,
photography, and more.

Also take a look at our highly
regarded art and literary journal,
Still Point Arts Quarterly, which
may be downloaded for free

www.shantiarts.com

www.ingramcontent.com/pod-product-compliance
Lightning Source LLC
LaVergne TN
LVHW020935090426
835512LV00020B/3372